DR RAYNOR BROWNE EL. LIBRARY
1000 N. MONTFORD AVENUE
BALTIMORE MD.
401 396 9239

CHILE
Where the Land Ends

EXPLORING CULTURES OF THE WORLD

CHILE

Where the Land Ends

Marianne Pickering

DR RAYNOR BROWNE EL. LIBRARY
1000 N. MONTFORD AVENUE
BALTIMORE MD.
401 396 9239

Benchmark Books

MARSHALL CAVENDISH

NEW YORK

> *The publisher would like to thank Linda-Anne Rebhun, Assistant Professor of Anthropology, Yale University, for her expert review of the manuscript.*

Benchmark Books
Marshall Cavendish Corporation
99 White Plains Road
Tarrytown, New York 10591-9001

© Marshall Cavendish Corporation 1997

All rights reserved. No part of this book may be reproduced or utilized in any form or by any means electronic or mechanical including photocopying, recording, or by any information storage and retrieval system, without permission from the copyright holders.

Library of Congress Cataloging-in-Publication Data
Pickering, Marianne.
    Chile : where the land ends / by Marianne Pickering.
        p.   cm. — (Exploring cultures of the world)
    Includes bibliographical references and index.
    Summary: Discusses the geography, history, people, and culture of this land of contrasts.
    ISBN 0-7614-0333-7 (lib. bdg.)
    1. Chile—Juvenile literature.   [1. Chile.]   I. Title.   II. Series.
F3058.5.P53   1997
983—dc20   96-19989
                                                                                               CIP
                                                                                                           AC

Printed in Hong Kong

Book design by Carol Matsuyama

Front cover: A young Chilean boy stands in a colorful cloak
Back cover: The Orsono Volcano near Ensenada, Chile

Photo Credits
Front cover: ©photographers/Aspen/Nicholas deVore III/PNI; back cover: ©Leo de Wys, Inc./Sunak Photo; title page: ©W. Hille/Leo de Wys, Inc.; page 6: ©Jerry Alexander/Tony Stone Worldwide; page 6 (inset): AP/Wide World Photos; pages 9, 29: Nicholas deVore/Tony Stone Worldwide; pages 11, 14, 53: ©David Ryan/DDB Stock Photo; pages 12, 25, 26, 30, 46, 48: ©Mark Harvey 1995/DDB Stock Photo; page 13: ©De Wys/Sipa/Kobbeh/Leo de Wys, Inc.; page 17: North Wind Picture Archives; page 20: ©Black Star/Christopher Morris/PNI; page 22: ©James Balog/Tony Stone Worldwide; page 28: ©Black Star/Michael Minardi/PNI; pages 32, 37: David A. Harvey/©National Geographic Society; page 34: ©Stock South/Andre Jenny/PNI; pages 39, 52, 54: ©Michael Moody/DDB Stock Photo; page 40: ©David Frazier/Tony Stone Images; page 41: ©Carl Frank/Photo Researchers, Inc.; page 42: ©Max & Bea Hunn/DDB Stock Photo; page 45: ©Buddy Mays/International Stock; page 50: ©Aurora/Jose Azel/PNI; page 56. ©1996 Artists Rights Society (ARS), New York/ADAGP, Paris

Contents

Map of Chile ....*Frontispiece*

1 GEOGRAPHY AND HISTORY
Land of Contrasts and Surprises 7

2 THE PEOPLE
One Culture, Many Roots 23

3 FAMILY LIFE, FESTIVALS, AND FOOD
Celebrating Family and Community 35

4 SCHOOL AND RECREATION
Time for Learning and Play 43

5 THE ARTS
A Nation of Artists 51

Country Facts 58

Glossary 60

For Further Reading 62

Index 63

Poet Gabriela Mistral was inspired by the beauty of the Chilean landscape and animals.

1
GEOGRAPHY AND HISTORY

Land of Contrasts and Surprises

La Divina

More than a hundred years ago, a child was born in a quiet village in northern Chile. She was raised in a small house made of sun-dried mud, close to the rugged and beautiful Chilean countryside. Her name was Lucila Godoy Alcayaga. No one then would have suspected that she would become one of the land's most famous and beloved poets.

Lucila was a religious child who felt close to the land and nature's creatures. She spent long hours in the orchard, talking to birds and animals and gazing at the clouds, the stars, and the changing waters of the river.

As a teenager, Lucila began to write poetry and stories. She described the valley of her childhood and the world of ordinary people. It was a world in which she found both beauty and suffering. She wrote about equality for all people. This made some Chilean leaders uncomfortable.

Fearful that her poetry might threaten her ability to earn a livelihood, Lucila decided to publish her writing under a new name.

She took her name from those of two of her favorite poets: Gabriele D'Annunzio and Frédéric Mistral. From that time on, she was known as Gabriela Mistral.

Soon, her writings were being published in many different countries and languages. In 1945, Gabriela Mistral became the first South American writer to be honored with the Nobel Prize for Literature.

Gabriela cared deeply about children around the globe. In 1946, she made the first worldwide request for money to help poor children. With this "Appeal for Children," UNICEF, the United Nations Children's Fund, was born. Today, UNICEF aids children in more than one hundred countries.

Gabriela Mistral was so admired that she became known as la divina *("the divine") Gabriela. When she died in 1957, at age sixty-seven, the government declared three days of mourning. Thousands of people crowded the streets of the capital city, Santiago, to attend her funeral. Today, her poems are learned by schoolchildren, and her words are celebrated in festivals all over South America.*

A Long Ribbon of Land

The scenes in Gabriela Mistral's poems describe a country of great contrasts. Chile (CHEE-lay) is shaped like a long and narrow ribbon. The average width of Chile is only 110 miles (177 kilometers). However, the country stretches along the western coast of South America for 2,650 miles (4,265 kilometers). It is almost as long as the United States is wide.

Chile has many different landscapes and climates. In fact, one can sample almost every environment on the earth's surface. From tropical regions in the north to the subarctic south near Antarctica, Chile has swamps and forests as well as glacier-covered mountains. It has rocky islands, volcanoes, and many unique plants and animals. One of the world's driest deserts can be found in Chile, as well as the stormiest coastline. Chile's rich agricultural regions provide delicious fruits and vegetables for people all over the world.

No one is certain how the country got its name. Some believe that it came from *chilli*, an Inca Indian word meaning "where the land ends."

Peaks of Snow and Ash

Nearly half of the land in Chile is made up of mountains. The Andes are a high, rugged mountain chain running down the western length of South America. It is the second-highest mountain chain in the world, after the Himalayas of Asia. Chile's Ojos del Salado Mountain is one of the tallest peaks in South America. It soars 22,539 feet (6,874 meters) into the air. Some of the majestic mountains of Chile are so tall and cold that they are covered with glaciers.

Steam billows out of the crater of an active volcano in Villarrica National Park in central Chile.

Chile lies atop one of the most active earthquake zones in the world. Almost daily, tremors rumble through the ground. More than one hundred major earthquakes have been recorded in the country since 1575. The city of Valparaíso has been destroyed by earthquakes five times in the past 200 years!

Earthquakes and volcanoes formed the Andes Mountains. This mountain building is still going on today. Active volcanoes, spitting smoke and ash, can be found throughout Chile. In Villarrica National Park in central Chile, vacationers can sometimes view white-hot lava flowing over the snowcapped peak of a volcano!

Not a Single Drop of Rain

The almost lifeless Atacama Desert lies in northern Chile. It is one of the driest deserts in the world. Some parts of it have never had a single drop of rain. Daytime temperatures are scorching, but the nights are extremely cold.

There is almost no plant life in the Atacama. Along the foothills of the Andes, the *cardón* ("candleholder") cactus manages to survive by absorbing water from fog that drifts off the mountain peaks. The tough outer shell of this plant is used by people in the region. They make window frames, doors, and furniture from it and use it for fuel. Few animals can live in this desert. One that can is the gray gull, which finds the desert a safe place to build its nest and raise its young. Each day, one parent flies to the ocean for food while the other stands over the chick, shielding it from the deadly sun.

Although the Atacama Desert has little life, it is rich in minerals. Vast deposits of copper, nitrates, and other valuable minerals are found in the region. They are sold to countries throughout the world.

The Valley of the Moon, in the Atacama Desert, is nearly lifeless, like the lunar landscape for which it is named.

The "Great Garden" of South America

In the middle of Chile, lying between the Andes and the Pacific coast, is a lush area known as the Central Valley. The country's heartland, the Central Valley is home to most of Chile's 13.8 million people. The largest cities—Santiago, Valparaíso, and Concepción—are all located in this region.

The Central Valley is ideal for farming, with its rich dark soil and abundant rainfall. Several rivers run westward from the Andes, bringing water and supplying hydroelectric power to the green valleys. Farmers grow great quantities of wheat and grapes, as well as oranges, melons, tomatoes, and many other crops.

CHILE

The fertile Central Valley produces a variety of melons, which are popular exports and are sold locally along the highway.

Cattle raising is also important. Ranches stretch for miles in the Central Valley. There are also large plantations of pine trees, which are grown to make paper pulp.

Chile is in the Southern Hemisphere—it lies south of the earth's equator. Its seasons are opposite to those in North America. When it is summer in North America, it is winter in Chile. The warmest months in Chile are between December and March. During these months, you might find fruits and vegetables from Chile at your local grocery store.

LAND OF CONTRASTS AND SURPRISES

The Stormy South

Chile's southernmost region is one of the stormiest places on earth. Severe winds blow without end, while snow and heavy, freezing rains fall almost daily.

Few people live here. In the milder inland areas, however, people raise sheep for wool and meat. Valuable deposits of oil and minerals have also been found in this area. And offshore are some of the world's deepest and richest ocean waters. They are home to more than 200 species of fish.

Southernmost Chile is a twisted puzzle of small islands and narrow waters. Huge colonies of penguins and sea lions blanket rocky terraces on many of the islands. Parts of glaciers break off and fall from high cliffs, crashing into the sea as

The far southern end of Chile is a land of ice and rock. Icebergs and glaciers, such as this one, fill the seas.

icebergs. At the southern tip of the continent, a steep and barren rock known as Cape Horn rises out of the sea. It is usually cloaked in fog and lashed by fierce storms.

Island of Stone Giants

Several islands in the Pacific Ocean are Chilean territories. Easter Island, about 2,000 miles west of Chile, is one of the most isolated places in the world. It was once covered with forests, but early inhabitants cut down thousands of trees and did not plant more. Today, most of Easter Island is only sparse grassland.

Easter Island has an ancient and mysterious past. More than 600 huge statues stretch in lines across the landscape,

Mysterious, giant stone heads dot a hillside on Easter Island.

standing like silent, watchful giants. In the language of the islanders, they are called Moai (moh-EYE). Scientists believe that they are between 500 and 800 years old. They think that the sculptures may have been images of ancient gods or ancestors. Carved from hard volcanic rock, some of the figures are taller than a two-story house.

Living in Wild Places

Isolated by natural barriers—the ocean on one side, the Andes Mountains on the other—Chile is home to a variety of unique animals. The world's smallest deer, the spike-horned pudú (poo-DOO), lives in the lush southern rain forests. It is only about 13 inches (33 centimeters) high. A newborn pudú could stand in the palm of your hand. There are also thick-coated llamas (YAH-mahs), alpacas (al-PAH-kahs), vicuñas (vee-KOON-yahs), and guanacos (GWAN-a-kos). These are all humpless relatives of the camel that are adapted to living in the cold, dry foothills of the Andes. For generations, Chileans have spun their thick, warm wool into beautiful cloth.

The skies of Chile are filled with hundreds of species of birds. There are pink flamingos, black-necked swans, colorful parrots, and jewel-like hummingbirds. Large colonies of penguins and other seabirds dot the long, rocky coastline. One of the world's largest birds, the Andean condor, soars high above towering mountain peaks. The largest of these birds can stretch its wings as far as ten feet wide.

Today, many of Chile's native creatures are in danger of becoming extinct, or dying out. The chinchilla (chin-CHEE-yah), a small rodent famous for its soft fur, has been hunted almost to extinction. The *huemul* (HWE-muhl)—a small deer that is pictured on Chile's coat of arms—survives only in a few places. Many animals and birds are threatened by air and water pollution. As more and more land is used for farming, mining, and forestry in Chile, the natural habitats of many species may soon disappear.

Chile's First People

Most scientists believe that people first arrived in Chile about 10,000 years ago. These early people moved from place to place, feeding themselves by gathering wild plants and hunting animals.

Archaeologists have learned many things about the early people of Chile from the tools and buildings they left behind. It is believed that about 3,500 years ago, for example, people in Chile began to plant corn and raise animals. Villages were built near the coast, where people could fish along the shore. Several different groups of people made the land their home. They built stone walls to protect their communities from attacks.

The Inca Empire

A powerful people in Peru, north of Chile, were called the Inca (EEN-kah), after the title of their king. He controlled everyone who lived in his lands. About 600 years ago, armies of the Inca Empire spread south from Peru, conquering the northern half of Chile.

The Inca learned some of their farming techniques from the desert people of northern Chile. From the Chileans, the Inca learned to grow crops on steep mountain slopes and in desert valleys. They built canals to bring water from the melting snow of the Andes Mountains down to the dry farmlands. Some of the canals built by the Inca stretched over very long distances.

LAND OF CONTRASTS AND SURPRISES

European Conquerors

Ferdinand Magellan, a Portuguese explorer in the service of Spain, was the first European to see Chile, in 1520. Within twenty years, Spanish armies using horses and guns—both unknown to the Indians—had conquered the Inca and many other peoples in surrounding regions. But they had not conquered the Inca and other peoples who lived in Chile.

In 1535 the Spanish king Charles I ordered Diego Almargo, an explorer, to find the best route into Chile to conquer that land. But once Almargo and his troops got there, they were shattered in battles with a fierce and ancient people—the Mapuche. After two years, Almargo and his few remaining men left Chile.

Another Spaniard, Pedro de Valdivia, designed a new plan to claim lands in Chile. He decided to start a Spanish settlement. In 1540, Valdivia marched into Chile with 150 Spanish soldiers and Peruvian warriors. He also brought Indian women from Peru and Catholic priests.

Traveling along the coast, Valdivia's men killed most of the people they met. Many people fled to escape the Spanish troops. By February 1541, Valdivia had reached a hill in central Chile. Here, he founded Santiago. Other Spanish settlers soon arrived in the new colony.

The Spaniards introduced horses to South America, which helped them defeat the Indians, who fought on foot.

Life under Spanish Rule

Their colony established, the Spanish invaders settled down to govern their new lands. European rule changed life in almost every way for the people of Chile and throughout South America. Indians—a term referring to the native people of the region—were put to work for the Europeans. They built cities, tended farms, and worked in silver and gold mines.

The early Spanish rulers were more interested in getting rich than in caring for the local people. Thousands of Indians died; many starved or were worked to death. Hundreds of thousands died from diseases that were brought from Europe, such as smallpox, measles, and influenza.

Roman Catholic missionaries traveled from Spain to teach the Indians their Christian faith. The Indians believed that spirits were everywhere. They worshipped many gods. Under the Spanish, however, Indians who continued to worship their old gods were punished or killed. Yet many traditional beliefs survived. In many cases, the old and the new religions became mixed together.

The Struggle for Independence

Chile was a Spanish colony for almost 300 years. In the early 1800s, independence movements developed all over South America. Early revolts in Chile against the Spanish were not successful. However, Chilean patriots eventually joined forces with José de San Martín, an Argentinean. He offered to help the Chileans.

San Martín knew that Spanish power in South America depended on control of Peru. Before South Americans could be free, the Spaniards would have to be driven out of Peru. He decided on a bold plan. He would march an army from

Chilean Government

Today, Chile is a republic. It has a written Constitution that protects citizens' rights and describes the responsibilities of the government.

The government of Chile is headed by a president, who is elected for one term of six years. The presidency is a very powerful position in Chile. The president helps design laws and appoints court judges.

Chile's laws are written and voted upon by the Congress. This body meets in the city of Valparaíso. Congress is made up of two houses: the Senate (with 48 members) and the Chamber of Deputies (with 120 members). Senators serve for eight-year terms and deputies for four-year terms. Eight of the Senate's members are not elected by citizens. Instead, they are named by the president.

The judicial branch is made up of the Supreme Court, nine Courts of Appeals, and lower-level courts. The thirteen judges of the Supreme Court protect the people's rights by deciding whether laws passed by the president and Congress are legal according to the rules of the Constitution.

The voting age in Chile is twenty-one. All citizens who can read and write are required by law to vote. People who don't vote must pay a fine.

Argentina, across the Andes Mountains, and into Chile. Once Chile was free, they would go by sea to attack Peru.

In 1810, Chile declared its independence from Spain. After many hardships, in 1817, San Martín's army reached the Central Valley of Chile. The Spaniards were taken by surprise and quickly surrendered.

San Martín appointed one of his Chilean officers, Bernardo O'Higgins, as the head of Chile's new government. The son of an Irish immigrant to Chile, O'Higgins is considered the father of Chilean independence. O'Higgins wanted to improve living conditions for all the people of Chile. He built schools, roads, a library, and a sewage system for Santiago. But wealthy landowners did not approve of O'Higgins's plans. In 1823, they forced him to leave Chile.

Civil war eventually brought victory to the wealthy landowners. In 1833, they adopted a Constitution that gave only

Pinochet and his soldiers ruled Chile between 1973 and 1990.

a few privileged people like themselves the right to elect the president and other government officials. The landowners thus protected their wealth and power.

Powerful Presidents

As the 1900s began, Chile looked forward to a prosperous future. But power to control the government remained in the hands of a few wealthy landowners. In 1925, a new Constitution was written. Every adult Chilean who could read and write was now allowed to vote in elections. Finally, Chileans could choose the people who would govern them.

In 1970, Chileans elected Salvador Allende Gossens as president. (Like many Chileans, he had two last names. The middle part of his name, Allende, was the name of his father's family. This is the name that most people use. The last part, Gossens, was the name of his mother's family.) President Allende (ah-YEN-day) believed that ownership of land and other property should be shared more fairly among all Chileans. His government took some lands from the wealthy and divided them among poor farmers.

Allende's plans were not as successful as many people had hoped. Chileans who had lost property refused to support the president. And without their money and skills, conditions worsened. Fewer crops were grown. Shops ran out of many goods. Workers were often not paid. Fights broke out in the streets.

The leader of the army, General Augusto Pinochet Ugarte, formed a military group, called a junta (HOON-tah), to take over the government by force. On September 11, 1973, troops loyal to General Pinochet (pee-no-SHAY) attacked the offices of President Allende. When the fighting was over, President Allende was found shot dead.

The military junta closed Chile's Congress within hours. It cancelled all elections. General Pinochet became president, but he was really a dictator. Citizens were not allowed to criticize him or the men in his junta. Books that spoke out against the new government were burned and the authors were punished. People who opposed Pinochet were often arrested. Many were tortured or killed. Thousands of people simply disappeared. They became known as the *desaparecidos* (des-ah-pa-re-SEE-dohs), the "disappeared ones."

Democracy Returns

Finally, in 1988, Pinochet allowed an election. The people of Chile could vote on whether or not he should remain president. As the election results were counted, it became clear that Pinochet had lost. A new leader, Patricio Aylwin (AIL-win), was elected president. He took office in 1990. However, General Pinochet kept control of the army. In 1993, another election gave the presidency to Eduardo Frei Ruiz-Tagle. It was another peaceful and democratic transfer of political power.

Presidents Aylwin and Frei (FRY) have worked hard to make Chile a peaceful democracy again. They have given the people back their constitutional rights. After years of violence and terror, the many freedoms of democracy have once again taken hold.

Indians, such as this shepherd in the Andes Mountains, were the original inhabitants of Chile.

2
THE PEOPLE

One Culture, Many Roots

Chileans are united by a shared history, language, and religion. Their roots are found in both South America and Europe. The blending of traditions from these two continents has created a uniquely Chilean way of life.

Mestizos

Few women came to Chile with the early European settlers. Spanish men married Indian women. Their children and their descendants were called mestizos (mez-TEE-sohz), which means "mixed ones." Today, about four fifths of Chile's 13.8 million people are mestizos. They have a mixed heritage, with both Spanish and Indian ancestors.

Europeans and Other Immigrants

Because of the country's remote location and natural barriers, fewer foreigners settled in Chile than in other parts of the Americas. People from regions other than Spain, however, have come to Chile. During colonial times, slaves from Africa were brought to Chile in chains. Their descendants often married Indians and Europeans. Today, little remains of African culture in Chile.

In the 1800s and early 1900s, small groups of Germans, Yugoslavians, French, Italians, and Swiss also made the long journey to Chile. Unlike the African slaves, they came by choice. They sought good jobs and a better way of life. Emigrants from England, Ireland, and Scotland also arrived in Chile. The Europeans were educated people who brought important skills to Chile. Some groups settled with their fellow countrymen in small communities, where they maintained the traditions of their past. Most adopted Chilean culture, giving up their old ways or blending them with ideas from their new home. Today, their descendants make up about one fifth of the population.

Following World War II, many people of the Jewish faith fled Europe to start new lives in the South American nation. Over the past fifty years, however, most immigrants to Chile have come from countries in the Middle East. Many of these newcomers began their own small businesses in their new homeland and prospered.

Indians

The original inhabitants of Chile included the Atacameno and Diaguita Indians. They lived in the Atacama Desert region in the north. The Mapuche lived south of the Central Valley. The Ona and Yahgan tribes lived in the far south.

Indian populations in Chile were never very large, but they were much greater before the Europeans came to their land. Today, Indians make up only a small percentage of the population. Some Indian groups, such as the Ona and Yahgan, are rapidly nearing extinction.

The Mapuche and other Indian tribes have frequently felt that the Chilean government has treated them badly. Many Indians have been moved from their homelands to less desirable places.

United in Faith

Most Chileans are united by a common religion: Roman Catholicism. While most do not attend religious services regularly, they consider themselves a

These Mapuche Indians use the horse as a means of transportation.

Catholic people. Religious practices like baptism, first communion, weddings, and funerals are important family events. Many children attend Catholic schools. Catholic priests and nuns are highly respected in Chile and have a tradition of working to help the poor.

Other Chileans are members of different Christian groups. There are also small Jewish, Muslim, and Buddhist communities.

CHILE

Many Mapuche Indians still follow some of their traditional beliefs. They believe that their God, *Guinechen* (gwen-EY-shen), created people and controls the forces of nature. The Mapuche also believe that spirits inhabit natural things, such as trees, stones, and the wind. Some Mapuche feel that Catholic saints hold magical powers. They make offerings to them at small shrines. The Mapuche have long believed that sickness is caused by the ill will of someone. A traditional healer, or *machi* (MAH-chee), still helps cure illness and gives blessings to crops.

A rural worker loads red chili peppers that have been dried in the sun.

Rich and Poor

In Chile, most property and money are in the hands of a small group of people. Most of these wealthy Chileans are descendants of Europeans. Some still own land granted to their families by the king of Spain more than 400 years ago.

Many people in Chile are well educated. They have skilled jobs in manufacturing, provide professional services, or work in the government. Some have started small businesses of their own. These Chileans usually own or rent a small house or apartment. While they are not rich, they live comfortably.

Most of Chile's poor people have little education and few job skills. Those who can find jobs often work in factories or on small farms.

City Life

Most of Chile's people live and work in cities. In the last one hundred years, many people have left the farms and other rural areas to seek jobs in the cities.

About 40 percent of the people in the country live in or around the capital, Santiago. Now the fifth-largest city in South America, Santiago is facing some of the problems that plague the world's other big cities. For many people, especially the poor, housing is hard to find. Because of the danger of earthquakes, few high-rise apartments have been built. Traffic chokes the city's streets. Air pollution is so bad that many people wear surgical masks when they go outdoors.

Santiago is home to Chile's richest and poorest people. Wealthy people often have servants to care for them in their luxurious homes. By contrast, about 1.5 million people are crowded together in slums. They live in shacks made of cardboard and tin scraps. Although some of these dwellings have electricity, most do not have running water. People must carry their water for long distances.

Northwest of Santiago is Valparaíso, Chile's largest seaport and second-largest city. It is built on a hillside overlooking the Pacific Ocean. The city has two levels, connected by steep stairways and public elevators. The lower part of

The lights of downtown Santiago twinkle in the darkness.

Valparaíso, known as the Basin, is used for business, manufacturing, and transportation. Railway lines and cargo ships meet at the waterfront. From here, many of Chile's products, such as fruits and other crops, fish, lumber, minerals, and machinery, are shipped all over the world. The upper portion of Valparaíso is the residential area. Twisting streets hold a mixture of stately mansions and tiny shacks.

Not far from Valparaíso is Chile's favorite resort city, Viña del Mar. The city's mild climate, beaches, hotels, and nightclubs make it one of the most popular vacation spots in South America.

Concepción, located on Chile's central coast, is a major industrial center. Its oil and steel industries attract many people looking for jobs.

ONE CULTURE, MANY ROOTS

Living in the Country

Traditionally, rural Chileans have lived and worked on large farms called *fundos* (FOON-dohs). In exchange for a portion of crops, tenant farmers worked for the owners of the *fundos*. Farm families often rented a small one- or two-room house on the *fundo*.

Today, many farmers work together in a business called a cooperative. They combine their crops and sell them together. This way, each farmer often makes more money than would be possible by selling the crops individually.

Some Mapuche Indians have moved to cities to find jobs. Many, however, still live near their traditional lands. Most rural Mapuche have modern homes, but some still live in traditional houses called *rukas* (ROO-kahz), which look a little like haystacks. Their low wooden walls and peaked roofs are covered with thatch made of sticks and straw. Inside, a handmade rug often covers an earthen floor. A fireplace is used for cooking as it heats the single room where everyone sleeps.

Farm life can mean hard work—even for children—but there's always time to have fun.

The World of Work

Chileans are a hard-working people. In many poor families, often even the children must go to work. In Santiago and other large cities, people usually work from 9 A.M. to 6 P.M., five or six days a week. Businesses are open half a day on Saturday, and everything is closed on Sunday. Men have traditionally earned the money to support their families, but now many women work outside the home. Many hold important jobs in government, education, and business.

About 17 percent of Chileans work on farms. More than forty countries buy Chile's grapes, apples, peaches, and other fruits. Families of agricultural workers move about throughout the year, harvesting whatever crop is in season.

Fishing is another important industry. Most fishermen work long hours for nine months of the year. They stay home

Fishermen often paint their boats bright colors and sometimes add pictures of fish or other decorations.

during the winter, when the weather is too stormy for boats to sail. Many women living along the coast are employed in factories where seafood is frozen, canned, or smoked. It is then shipped all over the world.

The mining of copper, iron, and other minerals provides work for thousands of Chileans. Since theirs is a difficult and dangerous occupation, miners are among the best-paid laborers in Chile. They can often afford comfortable houses with modern appliances.

Dressing, Chilean Style

Appearance is important to most Chileans. They take great care to be clean and neatly dressed. Most people in Chile dress in the same way that people in North America do. Men often wear suits and ties, while women wear dresses. Chileans dress up to visit someone's home or to eat at a restaurant.

Most schools require that students wear uniforms. Out of school, many young people wear neat blue jeans and shirts. Sloppy or torn clothes are not worn in public. People usually wear shorts only at the beach, not in town.

A well-known outfit in Chile is that of the *huasos* (WHA-sohs), or cowboys. Many horsemen wear clothes handwoven from the silky hair of llamas or guanacos. They wear short, brightly colored cloaks called *mantas* (MAHN-tahs). A *manta* is made from one piece of cloth with a hole cut in the middle for the head. It keeps the rider warm and dry while leaving the arms free to work with horses and cattle. A flat-topped hat with a broad brim shields the eyes from sun or rain. It is held tight with a chin strap. The *huasos'* pants are covered by long leather leggings, which are fastened with buckles and long tassels that hang to the ground. The *huasos* are also

This Mapuche Indian woman wears a beautiful and elaborate necklace made of silver coins.

known for their pointed boots and large spurs. Traditionally, these spurs were as big as saucers and had dozens of sharp points. They are smaller today, but *huasos'* spurs are still decorated with fancy designs and are often a source of personal pride.

Traditional women's clothing includes a full skirt worn with a long-sleeved jacket or blouse. A shawl or blanket, usually red or dark blue, is knotted around the shoulders. The women wear their hair in two long braids down their back, with a simple comb ornament on top.

In Chile, metal decorations are popular. Silver jewelry is worn by people of all backgrounds. The Mapuche have a long history of metalworking. In addition to crafting jewelry from silver, their ancestors used gold, copper, and tin. Large, circular silver pendants are worn by important Mapuche men. Bracelets and rings are worn by both men and women. Mapuche women often wear a chain with coins and pendants attached across their forehead or as a necklace. *Huasos* use these chains as decorations and reins for their horses.

SAY IT IN SPANISH

Here is how you would say some common words and phrases in Spanish.

How are you?	*¿Como está usted?* (KOH-moh es-TAH ooh-STED)
Nice to see you.	*¡Gusto de verte!* (GOO-stoh day VER-tay)
Yes.	*Si.* (SEE)
No.	*No.* (NO)
Please.	*Por favor.* (por fa-VOR)
Thank you.	*Gracias.* (GRA-see-ahs)
I'm sorry.	*Lo siento.* (lo see-EN-toh)
What is your name?	*¿Como se llama?* (KOH-moh say YAH-mah)
See you later. (So long.)	*Hasta luego.* (AH-stah loo-EGG-oh)
Good-bye.	*Adiós* (a-dee-OHS)

[Chileans often use the Italian word for good-bye, *ciao* (CHOW), instead of the Spanish *adiós*.]

The Languages of Chile

Spanish is the official language of Chile and is spoken by almost everyone. The Mapuche speak their own language, Araucanian, but also know Spanish. People on Easter Island sometimes speak Pascuense, a traditional Polynesian language. Immigrants from non-Spanish cultures may use their own languages at home, but Spanish is spoken at work, while shopping, and at school. Sharing a common language has helped Chileans to develop similar attitudes and values.

Chileans also communicate without words. Greetings, for example, are very important. Chileans believe that one should show respect for people and make them feel welcome. The *abrazo* (ah-BRAH-soh) is the most familiar greeting—a warm handshake and hug, and sometimes a kiss on both cheeks. When parting, the *abrazo* is repeated to say good-bye.

Llamas are often decorated for festivals in Chile.

3
FAMILY LIFE, FESTIVALS, AND FOOD

Celebrating Family and Community

Family comes first for most Chileans. People usually live with or near their extended families—parents, children, grandparents, aunts, uncles, and cousins. These family members are considered trusted friends as well as relatives. They spend most of their free time together. Holidays and other special occasions bring everyone together to share food, news, and memories. Community festivals also unite Chileans by celebrating people's shared traditions, values, and beliefs.

Family Connections

The father is usually the leader in the Chilean family. He earns money for the family's needs and makes most important decisions. While many women have joined the workforce in Chile, their main role is usually to take care of the home and family. Most Chilean men do not help with household chores and child care. At mealtimes, men are often served their food first.

Children—especially daughters—often live with their parents until they get married. Couples often date for several years before getting engaged.

Most marriages in Chile are performed in a Catholic church. Weddings are usually small and simple. During the ceremony, the bride's parents stand beside her and the groom's parents stand beside him. Wedding parties for relatives and friends are usually held at home. A light meal with wine and cake is served while guests dance to music played by neighborhood musicians.

Even after they have grown up, married, and started their own families, Chileans respect the elderly and listen carefully to their advice. Older people often live with and are cared for by their grown children. People also have a strong sense of duty toward their parents.

When a family member dies, the body is kept at home for several days. Friends and relatives visit, offering prayers and saying good-bye to their loved one.

Growing Up in the Catholic Church

The Roman Catholic religion requires children to go through several ceremonies before they can become full-fledged members of the Catholic Church. Infants are baptized in the first of these ceremonies when they are about two months old. A first communion takes place at the age of eight. Confirmation takes place when a child is a teenager.

Most holidays in Chile are religious ones. On Christian holy days, people attend mass, a religious service, and eat special foods. Many of these holidays are celebrated with a combination of Spanish and Indian traditions. Festivals held in honor of the holy days usually include processions in which religious statues are carried in the street. In these parades, people often wear traditional masks and dance to music played on folk instruments.

CELEBRATING FAMILY AND COMMUNITY

These motorcyclists prepare to ride in a parade for Quasimodo, *a festival that follows Easter.*

Easter is a time when Catholics celebrate Jesus's rising from the grave. In Chile, most families spend a quiet Easter Sunday in church and at home. On the following Sunday, Chileans in the Central Valley decorate their houses and hold a festival called *Domingo de Quasimodo*. People parade through town on horseback, bicycles, or colorful floats. Some people also bring communion—a service to commemorate Christ's Last Supper in which bread and wine are given to people— to church members who are sick at home.

Chileans honor important Catholic saints with special festivals. In Valparaíso and other port cities, the Day of Saint Peter is celebrated with a parade. Saint Peter was a fisherman who spread the teachings of Jesus Christ. Fishermen and others who make their living on water join together with brass bands and government officials to march from the center of town to the sea. Arriving on the shore, the people climb aboard boats decorated with flowers and flags to continue the celebration on the water.

Saint Anthony is one of the most popular Catholic saints in Chile. He is considered the shepherd of lost animals. He is also thought to help women find husbands. Each year on June 13, unmarried women visit shrines to St. Anthony.

Christmas: A Big Day

December 25, Christmas, is one of the most important days of the year for Chileans. Preparation for Christmas starts weeks ahead as *pesebres* (peh-SEH-breys)—scenes of the birth of Jesus—are created by folk artists. Carved of wood or made of clay, these nativity scenes show entire villages, complete with tiny people, animals, and angels. Set in the open doorways of homes, the small figures welcome visitors to enter and worship. Those who stop are often treated to *pan de pasqua* (pahn day PAHS-kwah), a special Christmas bread.

On the night before Christmas, people stay up late for the *Misa del Gallo* (MEE-sah del GUY-yo), or cock-crow mass. In churches all over Chile, thousands of candles glow as choirs sing and priests lead worshipers in prayer. Afterward, fireworks are set off in many cities and towns.

By this time, the children are falling asleep. They wake up in the morning to presents from *El Viejo Pasquero* (el vee-AY-ho pahs-KWER-o), the "Old Christmas Man."

December 25 occurs in the middle of Chile's summer. Many families celebrate with picnics on the beach. Some go to restaurants where they eat *curanto* (kur-AHN-tow), a dish from Chile's southern islands. It is made by roasting layers of eggs, vegetables, seafood, and meat in pits dug in sand.

These children are wearing festive traditional outfits for a parade.

Independence Day

Some Chilean holidays honor important events in the country's past. September 18 is Independence Day, when Chileans celebrate their nation's freedom from Spain. Crowds line the streets to watch parades of soldiers and military bands. People gather in parks and halls to dance the *cueca* (KWAY-ka), the national dance. Many Chileans drink *chicha* (CHEE-cha), a beer made from corn.

Chilean Foods

One of the most popular dishes in Chile is empanadas (em-pah-NAH-dahs). These are tasty meat pies, usually filled with beef, hard-boiled eggs, onions, olives, and raisins. Another popular food is *pastel de choclo* (pah-STEL day CHOH-klo)—a baked dish of beef or chicken, onions, corn, eggs, and spices. On festival days, many people enjoy eating

COOKING MANJAR

A favorite dessert of Chilean children is *manjar* (mahn-HAR). This delicious sweet is used as a spread for bread and cakes or as a caramel-like topping for ice cream.

You will need a 14-ounce can of sweetened condensed milk.

1. Remove the paper label and place the *unopened* can in a saucepan filled with water.
2. Over low heat, bring the water to a slow boil.
3. Boil the can for 6 hours, occasionally adding water so that the pan does not go dry.
4. Allow the pan, water, and mixture to cool.
5. Carefully, open the can and enjoy!

Safety in the kitchen is important, so be a careful cook and ask for help from an adult.

sopaipillas (soh-pie-PEE-yahs). The sopaipilla dough is rolled, cut into strips or circles, deep fried, and sprinkled with sugar.

Most meals are eaten at home. People usually have a light breakfast, perhaps toast and coffee with hot milk. The main meal of the day is eaten in the early afternoon. Many children come home from school to eat lunch with their parents or

Seafood is very popular in Chile, and many people shop daily for fresh fish.

grandparents. Tea and sweets are often served between 5 and 7 P.M. Chileans eat their evening meal very late, at 9 or 10 P.M. This light meal is a social time when friends and family gather together.

In Chile, meat is often barbecued or cooked in a *cazuela* (kah-SWAY-lah), a soup with vegetables, rice, and corn.

Chile's high-quality grapes produce some of the world's most popular wines.

Beans and potatoes are eaten with most meals. Seafood is popular everywhere. More than fifty varieties of shellfish are eaten in Chile! The favorite seafood dishes include *erizos* (air-EE-sohs). These are giant sea urchins, served raw or as a filling in pancakes. Another favorite is *caldo de pescado* (CAHL-do day pes-CAH-do), a seafood stew, which is served with hot, crusty bread.

Most people eat a simple dessert of fresh fruit. Custard apples, grown in the north, are often mashed, sweetened, and served as a refreshing drink. Coffee and tea, especially an herbal tea called *aguita* (ah-GWEE-tah), or yerba tea, are also popular drinks.

Chile produces some of the finest wines in the world. Most Chileans drink local wines with their afternoon and evening meals. Young children often drink wine mixed with water. As they grow older, children learn to judge the qualities of wines from different vineyards.

Most Chilean schools require their students to wear uniforms. These children have been having fun with face paint.

4
SCHOOL AND RECREATION

Time for Learning and Play

Education is highly valued by Chileans as the way to have a better life. They feel that it is the best way to prepare their children for good jobs. Many also believe that it helps move Chile forward as a modern nation. A shared knowledge of their common culture unites Chileans.

Preparing for the Future

Chile's schools are among the finest in South America. Almost everyone knows how to read and write. The law requires all children to attend school for at least eight years. Many young people also complete special job-training programs. A few go on to receive high school diplomas and university degrees.

Free education is available for all children between six and fourteen years of age. Many parents, though, work hard to pay for their children to attend private Catholic or other schools. Students in elementary grades study Spanish, math, science, social science, art, physical education, and religion.

In the seventh grade, students begin to learn a foreign language, usually English, French, or German.

In rural areas, children are needed by their families to work on farms or around the house. These students often attend school for only half a day.

Only a small percentage of Chileans attend high school or college. In high school, students study Spanish, reading and writing, citizenship, and math. Some students take courses in science, literature, foreign languages, or history to prepare for college. Others take courses that teach special job skills. They might learn how to use a computer, operate machinery, or repair cars and appliances.

For those who continue their education beyond high school, there are two well-known universities. One of the oldest colleges in South America was founded by the Spanish in 1758 as the Royal University of San Felipe and reopened in 1842 as the University of Chile. Here, students of all backgrounds attend classes to earn degrees in areas such as business, engineering, and medicine. Another very important university is the private Catholic University in Santiago, founded in 1888.

Taking Time Out

The people of Chile love to have fun. Popular activities include playing sports, attending the theater, listening to music, and going to the movies. Chileans spend most of their free time with their families. On weekends, relatives get together to enjoy large meals or to go to church. They also come together to play. Most people go on vacation with their families.

Chileans love the water. Most live only a short drive from the ocean, and many people can even see the water from

TIME FOR LEARNING AND PLAY

their homes. During the summer, Chileans often travel to resorts on the seacoast. Here, they swim, sail, water-ski, and fish.

During the winter, many people travel to the snow-covered mountainsides of the Andes, where they toboggan or ski down the slopes. The wonderful skiing conditions from June to September attract visitors from around the world. The most popular ski resort for Chileans is Farellones, less than an hour's drive from Santiago. Although skiing is very expensive, more and more Chileans are learning the sport. Some are even learning heli-skiing, which mixes skiing with hang gliding.

Thousands of Santiago residents enjoy kite flying on the weekends. Brought to Chile by Catholic monks more than 200 years ago, kite flying is popular with people of all ages. The skies are often filled with colorful, twirling shapes. Some

Chileans of all ages enjoy winter activities and sports in the mountains.

CHILE

fliers hold competitions where they battle to break the strings of challengers' kites. To do this, the strings are coated with powdered glass to sharpen them. Great skill is needed to snap the other kite free without sending one's own kite falling to the ground.

The National Pastime

Soccer may well be the most popular game on earth. It is most certainly the favorite sport of Chileans. Known as *fútbol* (FUT-bohl), soccer is widely appreciated. Professional players are regarded as national heroes and are among the most famous

A soccer match is played near the active volcano in Villarica.

TIME FOR LEARNING AND PLAY

people in the country. Up to 80,000 fans may fill the National Stadium in Santiago when an important match is held.

Twice a year, Chileans focus their attention on the soccer games played between Chile's two largest universities—the University of Chile and Catholic University. Shops and businesses shut down as everyone watches the match on television.

One does not have to be a professional or college player to be on a soccer team. Soccer games are played throughout Chile, in parks, school yards, city streets, and open fields. Young Chileans practice for hours to improve their balance and speed or develop new skills with the ball.

La Fiesta Huasa: Chile's Rodeo

Rodeos started during colonial times when Spanish ranchers rounded up their cattle once a year to sell. This was a time for celebration known as *la fiesta huasa* (lah fee-ES-tah WHA-sah). People from around the countryside would gather to watch cowboys show off their horsemanship skills. Over time, the rodeos grew into a contest, with strict rules that have not changed in almost 200 years. Chilean rodeo is an amateur sport. The *huaso* riders compete not for money, but for the love of the rodeo.

Chilean rodeos do not resemble the bronco-busting or steer-wrestling events of a rodeo in the western United States. In Chile, rodeos are held inside a semicircular fenced area. Wearing the traditional *huaso* outfits of *mantas*, fringed leggings, and large, multipointed, metal spurs, pairs of riders work together to guide a bull around the arena. Using horses as their only tools, the riders try to force the bull to stop at a certain place on the fence. This takes careful timing. The horses must be able to follow the rider's commands and make

CHILE

More than 400 years ago, the Spanish brought horses and cattle to Chile. Since then, rodeos have developed very specific rules.

sudden turns without angering the bull. Judges award points according to which parts of the bull are touched by each rider's horse. The team with the highest score is the winner.

Games Chileans Play

Every afternoon, in parks and fields throughout Chile, crowds gather to watch and play games. One of the most popular games is called *rayuela* (ray-WAY-lah). Heavy metal disks called *tejos* (TAY-hos) are thrown toward a string stretched across damp ground. Players try to throw the disk so that it lands on the string. The first person to hit the string a certain number of times is the winner.

In Santiago, adults often play this game on special public *rayuela* grounds. Children throughout Chile play their own version of the game using coins in place of the heavy *tejos*.

Another game enjoyed by Chileans is *chueca* (chew-AY-kah). The word *chueca* means "curved stick." This game was created by Indians long before the Spanish arrived in Chile. For ancient players, *chueca* was a serious contest between warriors. Today, children use a cane, a curved umbrella handle, or a hockey stick to play the game in parks and fields. A goal line is drawn across each end of a field. A hole marks the center of the field. To start the game, one player from each team tries to knock a small rubber ball into the hole. The team of the first player to succeed then drives the ball toward the goal. When the ball crosses the goal line, a point is scored, and the play starts again from the hole.

A less athletic game played by many Chilean children is called "*¿Quien Es?*" (kee-EN es), which means "Who Is It?" Someone is chosen to be the leader. Other players form a line behind the leader, where they cannot be seen. The leader asks, "Have you seen my friend?" Everyone answers, "No." The leader then says, "Do you know where he is?" The children reply, "Yes."

The leader then slowly walks forward for nine steps. Quickly and quietly, the other players move about. One player moves directly behind the leader. The leader then asks three questions to identify the player. He or she might ask, "Is it a boy or a girl?" "Is the person short or tall?" or "Is the person wearing red?" After three questions, the leader must try to guess who the player is. If the guess is correct, the person is leader again. If the guess is wrong, the player behind him or her takes the leader's place.

Many Chileans enjoy folk music. These musicians from southern Chile wear traditional outfits during their performances.

5
THE ARTS

A Nation of Artists

Art is an important part of Chileans' daily lives. Throughout the country, people express themselves in crafts, music, stories, and dance. Folklore is passed from generation to generation through familiar stories and songs. Many Chileans attend concerts, plays, and ballets. In Santiago, several museums collect and display art from Chile and around the world. Authors, poets, painters, and sculptors look to the capital city as a center of cultural creativity.

Art has also been used as a form of protest in Chile. Through their work, artists have expressed disappointment in their government and have encouraged social change.

Preserving the Ways of Long Ago

Many Chileans form links with their past through folk arts. Traditional crafts are sold in busy marketplaces and handicraft stores throughout Chile. Wool from sheep, llamas, and alpacas is handwoven by Mapuche women into colorful cloth used for cloaks, blankets, and sweaters. Mapuche artists are also known for their delicately crafted silver jewelry and for their musical instruments. Melodies from reed flutes and llama-skin drums are played on city streets as well as in quiet rural villages.

Some modern Indian artists create pottery in the same way that it was made hundreds of years ago. Clay is dug by hand from hillsides and riverbeds. It is shaped into a pot, bowl, or pitcher and then fired, or baked, in a large stone oven. The pottery is often painted with traditional black-and-white geometric designs. Some are decorated with handles fashioned into the heads of llamas and birds.

Stories in Cloth

In Chile, a colorful fantasy world is created from wool and cloth. Women embroider familiar folktales into beautiful scenes on cloth. These fine works of art are called *arpilleras* (ar-pee-YEH-rahs). A single cloth, detailed with thousands of stitches, can take an entire year to create. In one, a group of children stretch their arms toward a flying cow. In

Chileans have long used colorful embroidery as a way to tell stories.

another, a skeleton drives a garbage truck under a red sun. In a third, a woman sells fruits and vegetables as an enormous eye watches overhead.

During the dictatorship of General Pinochet, sewing *arpilleras* became a form of protest against the government. Many women made *arpilleras* that told the stories of their missing or imprisoned loved ones. Some of these *arpilleras* pictured families being frightened by soldiers with guns. Others showed prisoners behind tiny barred windows or women and children crying. "We embroider our problems," said the wife of a prisoner, "and our problems are ugly."

As Chileans learned about the stories on the *arpilleras*, they became angry at their president and his government. When elections were held in 1988, most people in Chile voted against him. The *arpilleras* had actually helped to force the powerful military ruler out of office.

A Santiago minstrel plays the charango.

Ancient Music and Joyful Dance

Chile's stories are also told in song and dance. Lively folk music is enjoyed throughout the country. Popular tunes are often played on instruments known to the ancient peoples of Chile. Although folk musicians play guitars, harps, and other familiar instruments, they also play traditional flutes, like *quenas* (KWAY-nahs) and *zamponas* (zham-POH-nahs). The

CHILE

charango (cha-RAHN-go) is a small, stringed instrument made from the hide of the *charango*, a small armadillo that lives only in the Atacama Desert.

Folk songs, called *tonadas* (toh-NAH-dahs), blend the melodies of Spain with the chants of Indians. A *tonada* is usually a slow-moving song with a melancholy theme.

Thirty years ago, the *Nueva Canción* (nu-WEH-vah kan-see-OWN), or "New Song," movement was started by Chilean musicians and poets. The writers protested against the government and demanded help for the poor. The songs are now popular throughout South America.

People dance the *cueca* at Independence Day parties, at weddings, and at rodeos. This folk dance tells a story of a rooster courting a hen. Accompanied by fast guitar music and tambourines, the dancers twirl their handkerchiefs while wildly stamping their feet. Spectators join in the fun—shouting, clapping, and keeping time with their feet.

A couple does the cueca, *Chile's national dance, at a festival.*

Chile in Arts and Letters

Alonso de Ercilla y Zuñiga (air-SEE-ya) (1533–1594), Spanish conquistador who wrote *La Araucana*, a long and famous poem celebrating the ancestors of the Mapuche people. Even though Ercilla fought bitterly against them, his poem describes the heroism of the Indian warriors who defended their lands from the Spanish invaders.

Enrique Soro (SOH-ro) (1884–1954), one of Chile's most famous musical composers. He wrote symphonies for orchestras and music for piano, violin, and cello. In 1948, Soro received the Premio Nacional de Art, an important national award. His music is well known in many Spanish-speaking countries.

Claudio Arrau (ahr-ROO) (1903–1991), outstanding Chilean pianist. Arrau gave his first public piano recital in Santiago at the age of five. Both as a recital pianist and as a soloist with major orchestras, he performed concerts throughout the world. He was widely respected as a player of Beethoven and other classical composers.

Marta Colvin (KOL-vin) (1917–   ), among the leading artists of Chile. She studied at the School of Fine Arts in Santiago and learned to create large sculptures in stone and metal. Her works represent Chile's varied landscapes and people. Colvin's sculptures are exhibited in parks and museums in South America, the United States, and Europe.

José Donoso (don-OH-soh) (1924–   ), an author whose work has been translated into many languages. His books tell stories from both real life and magical childhood dreams. One of his books, *The Curfew*, is about an artist who was forced to leave the country by the government. Donoso said that, in writing the book, he wanted to reclaim "the time that has been lost" during his own exile from his country.

Miguel Littín (Lit-TIN) (1942–   ), Chile's leading movie director. Littín was exiled during the rule of General Pinochet. In 1985, he disguised himself and returned to Chile. While there, he secretly filmed a movie about the cruel actions of the Pinochet government. His movie brought worldwide attention to the loss of democratic freedoms in Chile.

CHILE

This painting by Roberto Matta shows his dreamlike artistic style.

Artists and Authors

Chileans admire the arts of their European ancestors. For hundreds of years, in fact, artists in Chile looked to Europe for inspiration. Churches and government buildings, for example, were designed to look like those in Spain. Many religious paintings and sculptures were inspired and influenced by European artists.

In more recent years, Chile's artists have broken away from traditional European ways and have developed their own original styles. The best known among modern Chilean artists is Roberto Matta (MAH-tah). His paintings show imaginary worlds with bright, shining colors and dreamlike shapes. Matta's work is displayed in museums in South America, Europe, and the United States.

Over the past few decades, a number of Chilean authors have received worldwide recognition. Many of their books and poems have criticized the government. Poet Pablo Neruda (neh-ROO-dah) wrote about poverty, hunger, and the harsh life of factory workers in Chile. Born

July 12, 1904, he won first prize in a poetry contest at age seventeen. Pablo Neruda felt strongly that government should help the poor. Always involved in politics, he was elected to the Senate, where he spoke out on behalf of equality and freedom for all Chileans. Pablo Neruda made many powerful enemies. Finally, in 1948, government officials ordered the police to arrest him, but the poet fled before they could find him. He went from hideout to hideout, traveling by night.

Pablo Neruda was forced to leave his homeland. During his exile, however, he continued to write poems about the landscape and people of Chile. Around the world, people read Neruda's poems and demanded change in the Chilean government. In 1971, Pablo Neruda was awarded the Nobel Prize for Literature. When his friend Salvador Allende was elected president of Chile, Neruda was celebrated as a hero. He died just weeks before General Pinochet took power in 1973. Even after his death, Neruda has remained an important symbol of artistic freedom.

Another famous Chilean author is Isabel Allende. The niece of President Allende, she wrote a book that blamed Chile's richest and most powerful citizens for many of the country's problems. This and other of her works have become known and admired around the world.

Isabel Allende and many other authors were forced to leave Chile during Pinochet's rule. Their books could not be printed or sold in Chile. But they continued to write and found supporters in other countries. Through the power of their poems and stories, these artists touched the hearts and minds of millions and helped to return a sense of faith to Chile's people.

Country Facts

Official Name: Republica de Chile (Republic of Chile)

Capital: Santiago

Location: Chile is a long and narrow country that stretches along the southwestern coast of South America. It borders Peru to the north, Bolivia and Argentina to the east, Antarctica to the south, and the Pacific Ocean to the west.

Area: 292,058 square miles (756,430 kilometers). *Greatest distances*: east-west 236 miles (380 kilometers); north-south 2,650 miles (4,265 kilometers). Coastline: 3,999 miles (6,436 kilometers)

Elevation: *Highest:* Ojos del Salado, 22,539 feet (6,874 meters). *Lowest:* sea level

Climate: Chile has many different climatic regions. The Atacama Desert in the north is one of the driest places on earth. The fertile Central Valley is mild in winter and warm in summer. Southern Chile has colder temperatures, heavy rainfall, and strong winds year-round.

Population: 13,805,000. *Distribution:* 85.3 percent urban; 14.7 percent rural

Form of Government: Republic

Important Products: *Agriculture:* wheat, corn, grapes (for wine and eating), beans, sugar beets, fruit, beef, poultry, sheep. *Industries:* paper, textiles, appliances, food, and tobacco. *Natural Resources:* copper, coal, iron ore, lead, silver, gold, zinc, and nitrates

Basic Unit of Money: peso; 1 peso = 100 centavos

Languages: Castellano (Spanish), Araucanian, and Pascuense

Religion: 90 percent Roman Catholic, 7 percent Protestant, and small Jewish minority

Flag: The top half is white with a white star inside a blue square in the left corner; the bottom half is red.

National Anthem: *Himno Nacional de Chile* ("Chilean National Hymn") and *Dulce Patria* ("Sweet Country"), popularly known as *Puro Chile* ("Pure Chile")

COUNTRY FACTS

Major Holidays: New Year's Day, January 1; Holy (Easter) Week, April; Labor Day, May 1; Navy Day, May 21; Assumption of the Virgin, August 15; Independence Day, September 18; Armed Forces Day, September 19; Columbus Day, October 12; All Saints' Day, November 1; Immaculate Conception, December 8; Christmas, December 25

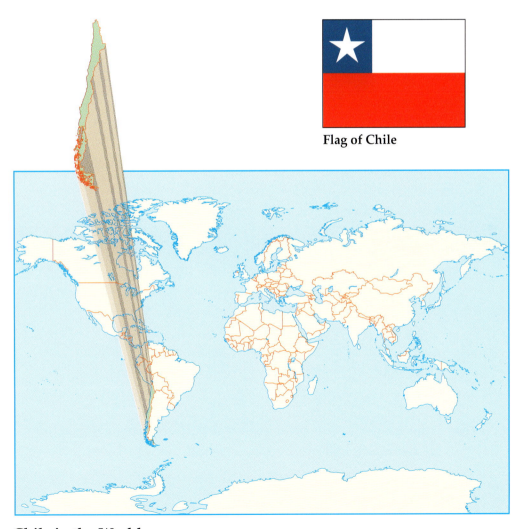

Flag of Chile

Chile in the World

Glossary

abrazo (ah-BRAH-soh): a greeting between friends and relatives that includes a handshake, hug, and kiss on the cheek

archaeologist: a person who studies the way humans lived long ago. Archaeologists dig up the remains of ancient cities and then study the tools, pottery, weapons, and other objects they find.

chicha (CHEE-cha): a beer made from fermented corn

colony: an area ruled by a foreign power

cueca (KWAY-ka): the national dance of Chile

culture: the arts, beliefs, and customs that make up a way of life for a group of people at a certain time

empanada (em-pah-NAH-da): a popular Chilean snack consisting of small pies stuffed with spices and cheese, meat, or seafood

exile: to send a person away from his or her country or home as a punishment

extinct: no longer active, as with a volcano; no longer living, as with a kind of plant or animal, or people

ferment: to cause a chemical change that results in the formation of alcohol. When juice from grapes ferments, it turns into wine.

GLOSSARY

fundo (FOON-doh): a large farm where tenant farmers work in exchange for a portion of the crops they raise

fútbol (FUT-bohl): soccer

huaso (WHA-soh): a Chilean cowboy or horseman

junta (HOON-ta): a military group that governs a country without being chosen through elections

mass: a Catholic religious service

mestizo (mez-TEE-soh): a person of mixed heritage; in Chile, usually a person with European and Indian ancestors

Moai: huge statues on Easter Island carved from volcanic rock by ancient people

native: one who was born in a particular region or country

nitrates: minerals that are used to make fertilizer and gun powder

rayuela (ray-WAY-lah): a Chilean game in which players throw a heavy disc at a string stretched on the ground

For Further Reading

Belting, Natalia M. *Moon Was Tired of Walking on Air*. Boston: Houghton Mifflin, 1992.

Carter, William E. *South America*. New York: Franklin Watts, 1983.

Chrisp, Peter. *The Spanish Conquests in the New World*. New York: Thomson Learning, 1993.

Haverstock, Nathan A. *Chile in Pictures*. Minneapolis, Minnesota: Lerner Publications, 1988.

Hintz, Martin. *Enchantment of the World: Chile*. Chicago: Childrens Press, 1985.

Huber, Alex. *We Live in Chile*. New York: The Bookwright Press, 1985.

Jacobsen, Karen. *A New True Book: Chile*. Chicago: Childrens Press, 1991.

Pitkanen, Matti A. *The Grandchildren of the Incas*. Minneapolis, Minnesota: Carolrhoda Books, 1991.

St. John, Jetty. *A Family in Chile*. Minneapolis, Minnesota: Lerner Publications, 1986.

Winter, Jane Kohen. *Cultures of the World: Chile*. New York: Marshall Cavendish, 1991.

Index

Page numbers for illustrations are in boldface

Alcayaga, Lucila Godoy. *See* Mistral, Gabriela
Allende, Isabel, 57
Allende Gossens, Salvador, 20, 21, 57
Almargo, Diego, 17
Andes Mountains, 8, 10, 11, 15, 16, 19, **22**, 45
animals, **6**, 10, 13, 15–16, 17, **17**, **25**, 31, **34**, **48**
Argentina, 18, 19
arpilleras, 52–53, **52**
artists, 55, 56
arts, **50**, 51–57
   as protest, 51, 52, 54
Atacama Desert, 10, **11**, 24, 54
Atacameno Indians, 24
authors, 55, 56–57
Aylwin, Patricio, 21

businesses, **12**, 27, 28, 30

Cape Horn, 14
Catholic University, 44, 47
Central Valley, 11, 12, 19, 24, 37
charango, **53**, 54
Charles I, 17
cities, 27–28, **28**, 29
climate, 8, 10, 12, 13
clothing, 31–32, **39**, **50**
Concepción, 11, 28
crafts, **32**, 51–53
cueca, 39, 54, **54**

Diaguita Indians, 24
democracy, for Chile, 21
Domingo de Quasimodo, 37, **37**

earthquakes, 10, 27
Easter Island, 14–15, **14**, 33
education, 25, 26, 27, 31, **42**, 43–44
embroidery, 52–53, **52**
emigrants, to Chile, 23–24

family life, 35–38, 40–41
Farellones, 45
farming, 11, **26**, 29, **29**, 30
fishing, 30–31, **30**
folk instruments, 36, 53–54, **53**
folk music, **50**, 51, 53
folk songs, 54
food, 36, 38, 39–41, **40**, **41**

games, 48–49
geography, 8–15
glaciers, 9, 13, **13**
government, 19, 20–21

history, 16–21
holidays, 36–39
homes, 27, 28, 29, 31
horses, 17, **17**, **25**, 47–48, **48**
huasos outfits, 31–32, 37, 47

icebergs, **13**, 14
Inca, 9, 16, 17
independence, for Chile, 18–20
Independence Day, 39, 54
Indians, 16, 17, 18, **22**, 23, 24–25, **25**, 36, 49, 52

jobs, 26–27, 30

languages, 33
llamas, **6**, 15, 31, **34**, 51, 52

Magellan, Ferdinand, 17
manjar, 40
Mapuche Indians, 17, 24, 25, **25**, 26, 29, 32, **32**, 33, 51
Matta, Roberto, 56, **56**
mestizos, 23
Mistral, Gabriela, **6**, 7–8

natural resources, 10, 13, 28, 31
Neruda, Pablo, 56–57
Nueva Canción, 54

O'Higgins, Bernardo, 19
Ojos del Salado Mountain, 9
Ona Indians, 25

peoples, of Chile, 16, 17, 23–32
Peru, 16, 17, 18, 19
Pinochet Ugarte, Augusto, **20**, 21, 53, 57
presidency, 19, 20–21

religion, 18, 25–26
   and festivals, 36–38
rodeos, 47–48, **48**, 54
Roman Catholicism, 18, 25, 26, 36–38, 43, 45
Ruiz-Tagle, Eduardo Frei, 21

San Martín, José de, 18–19
Santiago, 8, 11, 17, 19, 27, **28**, 30, 44, 45, 47, 49, 51
soccer, 46–47, **46**
Spain, 17–18, 19, 23, 26, 36, 39, 49, 54, 56
sports, 44–46, **45**, **46**

University of Chile, 44, 47

Valley of the Moon, **11**
Valdivia, Pedro de, 17
Valparaíso, 10, 11, 27–28, 37
Villarrica National Park, **9**, 10, 41
Viña del Mar, 28
volcanoes, 8, **9**, 10, 46

weddings, 25, 36, 54

Yahgan Indians, 24, 25

63

About the Author

Marianne Pickering has a degree in anthropology, the study of people and how they live, from the University of New Mexico. She has worked in museums throughout the United States writing and teaching about world cultures. She has written about education and growing up in Latin America in her children's book *Lessons for Life: Education and Learning*.

Ms. Pickering lives in Denver, Colorado, with her husband, Bob, and their daughters, Katie and Evie. She teaches third and fourth graders in the Denver Public Schools.